URBAN Words From A YOUNG Urban Poet

Urban Words From a Young Urban Poet

King Shawn Da Dawnn

Published by King Shawn Da Dawnn, 2024.

URBAN WORDS FROM A YOUNG URBAN POET

First edition. December 13, 2024.

ISBN: 979-8230032885

Written by King Shawn Da Dawnn.

Table of Contents

I wanted to dedicate Urban Words from A Young Urban Poet My Mentors & Professors & Teachers who never gave up on me even when I wanted to give up on myself. I dedicate this book to everyone who has supported me this far, coming to my events and reposting my open mic performances. You all are appreciated.

Acknowledge

"I would like to acknowledge all my poetry friends, family and supporters that continue to support me. I am thankful for each and everyone of you who has gone to my open mic events, like sharing and commenting on my social media posts and my mentors who helped edit my writing, giving me the foundation and knowledge of where to go to get my work out there. Thank You Luisa Paucchi, my fifth grade English teacher for keeping my poetry book safe after all these years. Thank You Salita Bryant for encouraging me to subscribe to Poets & Writers and where or how to submit my work for publication as well as prize submissions. Thank You Ms. Rozier for supporting me as a person first and then as an artist through all trials and tribulations. Thank You Family & Friends I created along the way".

This book is dedicated to
to that nikka
Who grabbed/Slapped my butt
The nikka who played around a little too much
When I had my last draw
That nikka who laughed a little too Hard
Or the one
Who kept
Popping that gum
Over
And Over
Again
After you told him to stop
Well...
"To: that nikka"...
I dedicated this to you
...Little did he know
that one day
I would get old
My heart
a little colder
...Old enough
Touch his his a-s-s
To let my Justice
Under God
Five shouts
4 rounds
one sound
Smoke him..
hear the sound

Of my Fear
go away
As my gat
Go
Pow!!!!
...Who could never get enough
attention
When the issue
Was never really funny
Well to that nigger
Suck on this B*tch
The cops want to come and want to call it "Virginia Tech"
This one is dedicated you
This book is dedicated to the millions of job applications
Those are thrown in the garbage
"Don't call us we will call you", or thank you for your time" as
you watch the time go bye
To the times you wasted on the people who don't care about
your kids,
You making your ends meet, a mother or father of three, with a
dead beat papi or mommy
Who only thing you got in common is the Maury or Jerry
Singer on TV
This book Is dedicated to the mouths you need to feed
The times they said they don't need you
F-you...let the well fare feed you,
All they give you is food stamps and a metro card.
This Poem is dedicated to
My Brothers and sisters who only decent income is selling crack
or giving blow jobs

Because hoeing and slanging is the only decent income
That comes in to keep a roof over your head
This poem is dedicated to
The men in jail
I don't have to be locked dup to know We're living in hell
The same rules that apply to you, apply to me
I just have a little more of what they call freedom
So Shut the f*ck up
Eat your lunch...
Mother Fu-ker
At least you get three meals a day
You eat Romen noodles...
Well... I'm eating roaches
Nikka I am starving
You want to trade...
Places?....Well Nikka...
Hear this...
I haven't had ...
A decent
Meal
In 44 days!
I lost my papi To Katrina
And the tsunami took my mommy
Hurricane sandy
Came in handy
Took my granny
And my auntie
And your bitch ass wants to complain
About commissary?
This middle finger is dedicated to

Them
They try to listen
To the diction or the content in how I speak
At a particular time, particular place
To have the never to judge me
To predict my future
And judge my flaws
I dedicate this middle finger to all of yall
You can lick an ass whole
More specifically, You can lick
Bits and pieces of sh*t, that I ate yesterday
To only find, the rest of me
Which was only mint to be
Flush down the toilet
Only to find out
I am not a misogynist
after all
The story is dedicated to
The Crips and bloods
Who always show love
To one another
Who are some of the best examples of loyalty
But who is A long distance cousin In reality
He who hold down the corner ever day at 2:30 sharp
Slap fives,
give pounds,
dap his bros...
Only to
Cut girls throat and little girls face
As a way to train b*t%$s in

Put them in their places

every 31st of the month

...Happy Halloween =)

....

But can never seem to show up for history

Class To learn the past

And change there future

For a better tomorrow

This one right here...Is for you

This poem is dedicated

To injustice I was severed

Who Never served my justice

At All

To Those substitute days

When it Was the worst day

When crime really does pay

He made the whole class laugh at me

And laugh, and laugh, and laugh

As he slap me in my face

To put me in my place

In the third, fourth or fifth grade

By Every single girl

I thought of

He made

Slap me too

because

they

Thought I was annoying

Or less important

And if I did something about it

If I stood my grounds
It was about to go down
Like a black kid
Who talk Lip
to his mama
or papa
From the projects
My bully said He hurt me
To my former
Abuser
A Toast!
"To Making me feel like the ugliest insecure little girl
... In the corner
That nobody thought of"

....

No bible, no scriptures
Could mend or content my broken heart
From seeing the smile on my bullies face
In the streets, in the class, around the school
Or on the corner
A Toast
To the times
He grew in power
as he picked on me
Every Single time..
The teacher left
For the bathroom
Out of the classroom
Or
Into the next room

"Imma Deck you?"

"What you looking at?"

To get a drink of water

Or

To call his/her daughter

But Ms. "Whats her face"

Ms. "Whats Her name" could not see

What was happening to me

I dedicate this to you

To every teacher, you turned their back,

why is it only that we say "F*%k the Police"?

To my brother from another Mother,

Who cut off the head of my Shaft

Who segregated my man's hood

From my Man Hood

For whistling at a light skin cute

Who was Hating on me,

Because I was trynna

To get the pum poo poona-neee

About to crack the da vinci Code

When he hit Coded red

Fake nikka

Who aint a nikkas

Just a B*%ch niggas

Time...wasted

Or snitch niggas

Chain Snatching

Lynched niKKa

Been a Nikka

Artificial Nikka

Why
are you here nikka?
Because
if a hater
Snatch a chain
nikka
It still won't free you
This chapter is dedicated to
To my beautiful rainbow woman
But not the of the rainbow flag
But of the different flavor
Like baskin in robbens
A beautiful creation when you come together
Stand beside each other
Black, White Orange Blue
This book is dedicated to
Who walks the earth with guilt
Who got me in my sleep
Forcing me to submit
In a dark alley,
Call the Police
But where I'm from
The Police
Never come
News camera man always run
And I am
Constantly reminded
Or ashamed
Of this guilt
I keep buried

Within
Because at the end of the day
I am
The only one
Who can fix it
This book is dedicated to
To my beautiful skinned woman
Locked down on lock down
Behind a Clear glass to make a phone call
Separated from love by silver monkey bars
The same monkey bars we use to swing on as kids
The same monkey bars
That brought once brought pleasure
Now brings me so much pain
Pain that I can't hold you
Yet
You are hell hostage behind a prison
Because you never listen
We could have worked it out
If you exchange words
Instead of weapons
Hold your head up
This book is dedicated to
The times I cried and cried dying inside
Forcing pills down my thought
Asking me questions,
Feeding me apple juice
To make the swallow sweeter
And or easier to swallow down
Bringing back up the memories

When my abuse
Was like apple
The color of p%$
This Joke is dedicated to the Jesus Jokers
Who always use the lord name in vein
You really want to preach!
Come tell that to my Home girl or Homeboy
Who is in cell block C
Preach to her/him while you're bent over
With your pelvis to the ground
Then manipulate the word of G-O-D
As somebody rump shake your town
This Verse is dedicated
To my brothers
And sisters
Dying of thirst
Dehydrated
And ready to swim
No, to dive head first
In a pool
Full of their own blood
This book is dedicated to
The decadence of nikkas
Who were once lenyched Nikkas...
The Lil nikkas
On the train
Who get on
Know my face
Cause I'm from around the way
I fit the description

I fit the profile, to the lil nikka
to the lil homiie
who know other homiies
It's about to go down
Hold up... wait....
is this racial discrimination???
Well to you Lil Nikka
I dedicate this to you
You who know my face from around the way
More than, you know an education
You who teach lessons, putting fear in my heart
Rejecting me, instead of protecting me
When we all for the same cause
This book is dedicated to the times I been through hell and
back
I could show you vultures
To
the times I yearned for a good laugh
A good cry
A good shout
To suppress the feeling inside
This book is dedicated to the man upstairs who goes by
different name
Some call him Ali
Some call him Jesus
Some call him a stranger
Some call him neither
But one thing is true
Love is a feeling, never given to abuse
Never given to be manipulated

Taken advantage of
Because In the end we are all God's children
Love is to Care
For God is Love
Rev, Good Speed...King Dawn

I made it up, in my mind, to "see you" next time I see you
    Next time I see you...
  Once, my eyes
  lock onto yours
  It's O-V-E-R
  Once I notice it's you
  Could be in the middle of the street
  The middle of next week.
  Head Crack!
  Bink!! BINK!
  Could be today.
  Right hook!! left jab!!!
  Could be tomorrow.
  Left hook! Right Jab!!
  If I even think about holding back
  Head Crack!!! Right hook, uppercut, left jab!

• • • •

CRACK! CRACK
  Bink Bink!
  Another blow to the head!
  You had to know I was coming for you for what you did.
  For what you did
  In public!
  In front Of me.
  You know like I know that you played yourself Kid.

. . . .

IT COULD BE TOMORROW, ten years from now when I stop by my momma's house for Family Dinner.

I'll even give you a 30 day to go learn and train.

Do what you need to.

PREPARE yourself For this ass whipping.

You SHALL RECEIVE!

The NEXT time WE MEET

I DON'T CARE!

I DON'T CARE!

You had to know I was coming for you for what you did.

You played yourself Kid

Could be in the middle of the street.

In the middle of next week.

OR Tomorrow on the corner,

Call the coroner at 4:15

I DON'T CARE!

I don't care

If I am in the middle of the Aisle,

Grocery shopping for VELVEETA cheese.

And it falls on a Sunday,

And you happen to sneeze in an Aisle full of children.

I DON'T CARE!

I AM GOING TO LEAN ONE IN bruh!

or

If I notice you're in line in front of me.

Paying for food, with your EBT, food card.

I'M STRAIGHT CRACKING YOU BRUH!

. . . .

WITH A CENTER BLOCK.
   Maybe a brick.
   Anything with a nice GRIPE
   That will Get the job done
   Real fast, REAL quick!
   SO LET YOUR PREACHES BE TO JESUS
   Pray he never SEES us. Meet.
   Because
   IT WON'T BE PRETTY my man.
   F%$k a "Please"
   F%$k a plead
   F%$k a plan B
   I DON'T CARE!

• • • •

BECAUSE
   I won't care
   Who there
   Who sees or
   Who C's me do IT!
   I just won't Care!!!

The clock has struck one
    Hooray! I have assignments
that has to be done.
It must be turned in???
It must must be turned in
Yes yes Double spaced
Times new roman font.
No coverages
Just written in MLA
with 5 inch margin
On all four corners
Maybe 2-3 pages
Maybe 4 pages
With a page number
Located at the top right.
I want go way up
Up above the clouds
Up above the mountain
Far beyond the sea
I want go way up
Up above the trees
Up above the trees
And stick
Like honey to the beez
I want to go Way up

Room 129/ The Counseling Center

A re you mad?
      Are you sad
Are you feeling blue
i got good new for you
Woopy te doo
You will be as good as new
Got a hunch on your shoulder
What are you going through?
What you going through?
I go through a lot? I got
Just flop a seat down on green couch
Are you going through alot of shhh?
I get
Room 129
They don't mind one bit
going through alot?
I definitely get it!
Room one twenty nine
They don't mind one minute
Are you worried about it?
It's complicated!?!
Don't procrastinate
just make sure you dedicate
Your time to counseling
Go go go inside
Inside the counseling center
Speak to a mender

All of your problems
Will disappear bottom line
Room 129,

Down by the Little Lake Road

Down Down by the little lake road
If you in a pickle don't worry
Down Down by little lake road
There is so much to see
Down Down by little lake road
IF U wanna see a shits show
You can find everything you need
Down Down by the little lake road
There's monkeys doing back flip
Down Down by the little lake road
Theirs aunties frying chicken
Extra large napkins
Down Down by the little lake road
Their was pancakes and Jimmy Dean sausage
And pickled pig feet with roasted asparagus
Down Down by the little lake road
Porkchops with gravy, collard green
Yams potatoes and fish fries
Down Down by the little lake road
From 2022, 2002,1962 to 1902
Down Down by the little lake road
Peter, Piper, Pecked a Peck of Pickled live your life
Down Down by you get the point

I'm Harlem's Nephew
   That Young King
Cheese spot, Fried Chicken, KFC
That Big Mac, Philly Cheese Steak
Take the Cake, eat it up in your face
New Beginnings
I Got friends
Square Root of Four, is Two Man.
That Orange Soda
That Sunkist
12 ounce can soda Boy We Reminisce.
On The Good day...
Call it Corn rolls
Strolling down 42nd with a dollar for Doritos.
I Study Hard Books & Pens.
Highlighters. Concentration. Yeah I'm focused Man.
I'm Harlem's nephew.
That young king.
Cheese spot, Fried chicken... philly Cheese
I'm Harlem's nephew.
That young king.
Cheese spot, Fried chicken eating KFC.

P-i-z-z-a
SAUCE, cheese, DOUGH, pepperoni.
May I have a slice.

Where Walnuts Whisper

It is very hot
Crop tops and mitch match socks.
Deep fried tater tots.
Sweating bacon greece.
Bacon greece and Philly cheese.
Philly cheese and chips.
music is blasting.
Asses is clapping left right.
Not a care in site.
Hot dogs are boiling.
Kool Aid's pouring in cups.
Rump shake your butt butt.
Chili cheese & french fries.
Sweet potato no pumpkin pies.
Fresh out the oven.
Brown yellow muffins.
Cootie cutters no bow ties.
Tickle me elmo.
Da Da Da Da Da Dora the explorer
Passing me right by.

We were 2 heart beats
    Ba ba-boom
Intertwined
Look me in my eyes
Tell me where was the lie?
Long talks we'd talk on the phone
There wasn't a discussion where we wouldn't go
Extensive phone calls and phone bills
Facetiming that babyface you had that whip a peal
Don't understand how hard it was to let you go
Holding on to something, A love that wouldn't grow
You use to be there for me when I fall
When they smirked you told me forget them all
And Now on your knees
Baby, please, Don't,Baby please!
Latching onto "He"
When you took advantage of me...

A Dead End Job

Her tears are a dead end Job
No room for growth in her company
All it does is take up my time
I got other priorities
I clock in and out everyday
For my pay
And still ask me to do more
My hands got blisters, my feet are soar
I break my back and all that
Just to keep the tears a success
While they put a price on my head
Then make bets to see what they can get
Outta me
Im done
Fuck them tears
I don't care
Mans greatest weakness
Is them got damn Tears
So Imma go back and read
How to succeed
Study a my craft, to be
Come The master, of my own destiny
Her tears are a dead end Job
Her tears are a dead end Job
When I get sick, I try to call in
This B#%ch has a fit
Man Im sick of this sh%t
She Wanna cut back, on my hours
And already, looking somebody to take my place

The nerve of this b-i-t-c-h
(don't read aloud: I say, To myself, But no one else)
I worked my ass off
Blood, sweat, tears
For many long years
Do you even care?
Man F%$k them Tears
Her tears are a dead end Job
So Imma go back learn to read
to succeed
Study a craft that means the world to me
And become the master of my own Destiny

The Room was dark but just enough to see
The lights were low but comforting for me
The Music was playing while bodies conversed in conversation
I desired to kiss you here and touch you here
Yea
Just like that we undressed instantly.
Inside of my Mind
Where I swear we had reinvented sex 5, 6 7 times
I was kissing yours lips you were kissing mines
In this exact moment , place of Time
Our lips touch,
hearts raising,
a surge of energy
pass the lips from our faces and down our spine
I looked at you, looking at me
Then You whispered ever so soft into me
"Stay, Stay with me"
The music changed
Darkness turned to day
We had to part separate ways
cuz the party was over
What is your name?
Damn
No wait ...
"Stay, Stay with me"

SMILE

When we had CHINESE CHICKEN WINGS times was good.

When it was HARD TIMES, we had hot fries with hot sauce.

FRIES went a long way BECAUSE we all had about THREE or four.

As long as NOBODY put their mouth on the bottle NO BACKWASH!!!

Remember JOHN, Sandy and UNCLE Ben.

Like HOW YOU BEEN???

"Remember when"?

WAY, WAY BACK THEN!

You have friends.

YOU USE TO PLAY WITH THEM

I AM going BACK time

To find exactly where did I lost my smile

Talk is cheap so let my heart guide the way

The light is shining

The flames are lighted

And the music is blasting away

COME OUT AND PLAY!

Smile ONE MORE TIME

Smile AGAIN

I am going back in time
To find exactly where I lost my smile
That's been hiding for a while.
Letting my heart show it the way
Until it believes it can see the light.
I am teaching it to crawl, Before it walks
Build it up from the ground up
A lesson I was seldomly taught
Holding its hand
One step at a time
Baby steps, until it's fully grown
Until it confident enough to say daddy "I not a baby anymore"
And sit back like a proud dad
And watch its son rise and shine on the thrown
And walk the burning sand all on his own.

Smile JUST FOR ME
Where exactly did I drop it off?
Did I live it in the hands of a stranger?
Did I jeopardize my smile by putting in danger?
Is he under a tree?
Is he inside of me
Did I lose it to the system?
Did I let it play the victim?
Did I lose it to the hands of trust?
Or lust
Do I blame myself for it missing?
It's my mission
Lord as my witness
To find what been missing
Come Out and Play

I am from The city that never sleeps
   I am from the city of Bright lights
"Stand clear the closing doors please"
125th and Lexington
149th street grand concourse
Jacob Soulfood Restaurant
Famous fish fry
The taste will have you coming back for more
Im from the island of Baked Macaroni and cheese
Collard greens
Candy Yams
Peach cobbler
Sweet potato pie
Corn bread
Five guy 16 dollar cheese burgers
Harlem Hospital
Lincoln Hospital
United States Post Office
Channel 7 news
Fox 5
Im from "Let me get a Chop cheese on a hero,salt pepper, ketchup"
Bacon egg and cheese on a roll
Im from the Corner store
Bodega
Dollar pizza
Popeye

IHOP
DoorDash
Uber Eats

I am traumatized
by the phobia of seeing kids
with other kids
from unfamiliar places
Because in those moments,
the sun suddenly stop shining amazing graces
Everything slows down,
my vision gets blurry
then things turn heavy gray
for a second I worry
My mind goes into a trance,
my body begins to shake I begin to panic
paying close attention
to everything hes doing and what they are saying
My hat is low, I am trying to be cool
but boy im sweating
Cuz if he starts reaching,
the way their leaning
into each other sharing secrets
ooooh...my stomachs is queasy,
I don't feel like eating
im not speaking
I could feeling them getting closer
What is he smiling for?
I just want to go home
What is he smiling for?
Why wont they leave me alone?
What is he smiling for?
I find the strength to look back
They kids into the corner store

• • • •

I'M TRAUMATIZED BY the phobia of kids with other kidz in
unfamiliar places
    but what am I to do?
    I have to...
    how else am I going to
    get to where I need to?
    Phobia

Apartments For Rent

Need my own
Tide of coming home
and shit always go south
Somethings always wrong
Always a Huff and puff
A scream and shout
I looked on apartment.com
I looked on Craigslist
Tired of that bullshit
"You have to make 40 times the rent"
Wash the Dishes,
Clean out the tub
Mop the floor
F%#k these chores
Go to the store
Who works for free
Take out the trash
While you sit on your ass
Tired of you blasting music every single day
Playing the same old ass songs
You don't like closed doors
I don't want to hear nomore "Luther Vandross".
Give that shit a break
I wish sometimes had my own to slam this door right in your
fucking face.
Tired of walking on egg shells
I can't do this or you get mad
If I don't do this and this
You get mad.

Where is my Dad?

I didn't ask to be here

I'm not the one who open my legs

Excuse me I beg your pardin

I hate it here

I can't win for loosing

I can't breathe

I'm up to hear with your bullspit

Up to the knee

Always catching a fit

A f#$king fit outta nowhere

F$%k outta here!

F%ck outta here

You eat my stuff ...

You play the blame game saying you gave me life?

You aint buy this So you not trying this!

I can't live

Petty mother f$#ker you the worst kind of one

I need my own.

You Can't Eat at Everybody's House

This year Thanksgiving is going to be at Grandma Brison House.
She had warned me about House hopping.

People don't wash their greens.

Cooking Macaroni in the kitchen sink.

Making potato salad in the bathroom tub.

Folks not properly washing their chicken.

People be digging up their nose, and their ass and trying to fix me a plate.

You can't eat at everybody's house

Then people have the nerve to gossip about somebody.

What this person wearing

Why this person outfit don't match but smile in your face saying "you look good girl".

Talk about you like a dog .

You can't eat at everybody's house.

They don't put no loving in the food.

But question why you haven't ate off your plate.

Be careful with your white friends that swear they make a good green bean casserole with raisins in the potato salad.

You can't eat at everybody's house

Brother Belize

• • • •

I hope you put in a good word for me...

to the man upstairs

Hope you share the changes... in me...

that I can't see in myself

I never really believed in the cross...

until you cross my path.

...Oh Freedom At Last

YOU DIED IN YOUR CASKET like Jesus died on the cross.

    Almost like you died for our sins

    Then you died for a cause

    Like you died to make sure Jesus is real

    Then you died for a reason, to make sure he had

    Hear my cries

    Yet you lied

    Down peaceful at death

    But we all knew you suffer

    From stores about you in the hospital

• • • •

You flatline like Jesus

Then rose from the dead

Come back to send a message before

That green light straightened

YOU DIDN'T COME WITH no bible, no scriptures

    But you did want your people to follow

    So If your is like Jesus

    Then let me write your bible

To learn you ways
Teach them,
Before Judgment day...
You died in your casket like Jesus died on the cross.
Almost like you died for our sins
Then you died for a cause

You came back from a flat line
Like Jesus Christ come back from his children
Come back to send a message.
Before that last line finish

• • • •

I LOVE YOU, GOD KNOWS I do
    Now you're Free as can be
    Just hope you put in a word to Jesus
    to save a seat
    up in heaven...
    Just for me..
    Please..
    Brother Belize

Why I'm Never going back to Meekiee's House

Never have I been more afraid I my life
Cooka Ra Cha on the stove
Cooka Ra cha on the chicken
Cooka Ra Cha on the fan
One Cooka Ra Cha
Two Cooka Ra Cha
Three Cooka Ra Cha
Four
Cooka Ra Cha on the Ceiling
Cooka Ra Cha in the bed
Cooka Ra Cha in the Tub
Cooka Ra Cha making love
In the middle of the living room floor
Itchy for itches just thinking about it
With their big black bodies
1 Cooka Ra Cha
2 Cooka Ra Cha
3 Cooka Ra Cha
4 ...
Cooka Ra cha march me to the front door
He'll no I'm never coming back
I can't believe he offered me food
Cooka Ra Cha greeted me in the pot of Macaroni and
gon- do- less rice and beans
I'm never coming back

I'm sorry I walked away from you
Inseparable
Every song
Every INTRICATE beat musicality
A listening ear
I could still pick up
Every song reminds me
Reminds me of what we use to be
It still drives me crazy
A love that use to be
I did love you
Inseparable
Intuned
One with Gods
Inseparable
We were a team...
Dancing in the moon light
With my fresh sneaks, snap back fitted and new pair of jeans
Living in Every minute of it
Every intricate beat
Some nights I wake up and wounder why
Somewhere I got lost
Uncontrollable distractions
The selfish act of a stranger
Circumstances out my control
The best gift offered now is an acknowledging action of apology
A Distant Stranger now to me
Some nights I wake up in cold sweats wounder why
Tear drop away from a cry
I enjoyed your company

Oh how I enjoyed your company
Priceless
More than riches
Riches could ever buy
My twin
My safety
Why did we go wrong
Fallen off
Some days I wake up and yearn to be intune
In unison in one with the higher up
With one with God's
Wrapped in your arms
Infused in the moment
So appreciated
An acknowledgment to Every mentor
Every tutor
Everyone who ever believed in me
See I never knew where I was going to go
Or where it would take me
But I did it
with you
Without you I feel underrated stress misunderstood alone and at
time angry
at time alone and angry
Alone
Lonely
In lost of my form of communication
Default in Forbearance of my occupation
Every song reminds me of what use to be
being in the presents of in your company

True internal Exsticey
A form of communication that led to a love that could always see
and never gave up
on me
Ooh yeah yeah
Dear Dance & Artistry
Take this sincerity
Form of an apology
Sincerely an artist
By the name of .
King Shawn Da Dawnn

"November 17, 2024

I'm tear drop away from crying
A few shots away from dying"
Rent due, light due, Car note due
Baby need dippers, Everybody wants their payments
in full
Baby momma trippin
Courts think im slippin
Courts won't let up on payments
Incarceration or Facing Eviction
"Feel like you drowning in the Lords pain"
I still smile behind the pain
Walking around like everything been the same
And ain't a damn thing change
But to Still release it in the showers rains
How I feel? How it's been?
I haven't picked up a pen
I don't know, since God knows when
I haven't danced to a beat
I'm feeling weak
Siblings ain't been the same
Momma got needs
Baby brother ain't got it
Everybody thinks im good
nobody checking on me
I'm holding on by a thread
Sister won't let me in for a place to stay
It's pouring Rain
Dear Father,
Adulting has me neglecting my dreams
That You use to encourage me to follow them by any means?
I have resentment calling for your name
I don't know how to do it
My lady is unappreciative
Unsure of fame
if fame really for me?

Not being able to provide
With every smile , Feel like she is wasting her time
Trying to feed a family of three
On the count down
In the thick of it
At the end of it
Getting sick of every thought of me
And the mention of my name
Drowning in the Lords Pain
In the Heart of Chaos
The thought of you
Gives me strength
With every calling on you
A simple conversation
I Reprogram.
Did we last end on bad terms?
Was it me?
Was it something I did?
Let me know
I have resentment call for your name
These woonds keep bleeding
These woonds keep bleeding
But Father I'm tired
I call just to hear your voice
Who knew this would be in store for me?
In the Heart of Chaos
A release of
Word of affirmation
Drawn from your life experiences
Words of encouragement
To get me back in the game.
Because Who said, as a grown man you wouldn't need your father?

This Christmas (2007)
So we out to This Christmas
After playing footsie Lords my witness
You been a bad bish
Now the bad bishh is in detention
After chasing you up and down the hall
The hall
Breaking the forth wall
after every drill recital
Recitals,got me Reciting,
Reciting how you got me tight!
Oh my god!
Now Im, Reciting
how i can Drill you?
& Take you to school

• • • •

YOU BEEN A BAD BIISH
Now the bad biish is in detention
Getting hot, sweat blocks on and across your forheads,
On the forhead
While the screens dead
pushing, pulling,
More pulling less pushing
on each other clothes
Lord knows
Dipplets Dripping from between the seam of the inside of
those jean pants
On a weekend
a surge of energy

From the leaking
pass back a surge of energy from our faces and down our
spine.
Grip getting stronger on me
Feels for the night, best time of our lives
The movies over, twinkle all in your eye
Flashbacks of seeing you bent over not gonna lie
So we took each other up for the long walk home
I could give a damn about the popcorn
Temperature getting hot, It's getting hotter
110 degrees in the middle of December
Twinkle in your eye
Never told a lie
In the blizzard cold
In the blizzard cold
You been a bad bitch
Now the bad bitch is in detention
I lean in
Now im feening
Breath getting heavier
Your temperature rising from up under that sweater
Fresh manicure Nails digging into me
Flesh smooth as a new born booty
Feels for the night, best time of our lives
Sweet like chocolate kisses Lips so juicy

Letting My Beard Grow (L.M.B.G)
I've been slouching under the covers.
on tick tok.
Browsing Twitter post.
Liking pics.
on the gram.
Netflix,
Yea I been doing the most.
Scrolling through Twitter, for so long.
my thumbs gotten numb.
I've been f%$kin' cooped up
Yea, My thumbs gotten numb
I been in the bed
sipping eggnog
with fajitas,
Cocktails & Coquitos
Gaining that baby weight.
Eating syrup sausage, flap Jack's
eggs, steak, hostess cupcakes.
I've been feeling cooped up
Letting my beard and hair grow
Letting that laundry pile up but not today
Run that Back
Return the mack
Run that Back
Return the mack
I've been slouching under the covers
on tick Tok
Netflix, Yea I been doing the most
Letting that laundry pile up but not nomore

Not today
Run that Back
Return the mack
Pull out the jack & coke
18 Racks In my possession
we about to turn up for sure
Shave down the five o'clock shadow
Bring out the wardrobe
Shave down the five o'clock shadow
Bring out the wardrobe
Make sure my Cesar Fade is extra crispy
And Pull out the Giorgio Armani
Tonight's going to be a movie
We making a movie for sure

Don't miss out!

Visit the website below and you can sign up to receive emails whenever King Shawn Da Dawnn publishes a new book. There's no charge and no obligation.

https://books2read.com/r/B-A-KDVUC-ZJGIF

Also by King Shawn Da Dawnn

Urban Words From a Young Urban Poet

About the Author

Hey Yall! My name is Shawn Lackerson but I go by my pen name *King Shawn Da Dawnn*. Born in Harlem New York, raised in the Bronx but currently living in Miami Florida I have been training and performing since a young age winning first place in the 5th grade poetry slam competition. Since 5th grade I have developed a love for writing.

I discovered and developed all my love for poetry from my mother Ms. Lakerson. Since a young age I used to watch my mother write songs in her notebook. I was inspired by mother, who would also share her story of going to performing arts school in Manhattan, taking theatre classes.

I have had my work published in April 2024's Issues of *The Scene*, winner of 2023's *Alice Minnie Hertz Heniger Prize* for creative writing for best graduate creative writing in any genre & Honorable

Mention of 2024's *Writer's Digest* writing competition just to name a few.

I have performed at many open mics throughout NYC from places such as the *Nuryican* Cafe, *Harlem Bomb Shelter*, *Trouble Makers Open Mic*, *The Urban Juke Joint* & many others, currently in *Mellow Dramatic Mondays* by On the B Side Ent in Miami Florida.

Aside my poetry I enjoy acting, dancing reading, writing and listening to music. What every i endure in I definitely put my all into it.